God Knows Your Story . . .
(and He's Not Mad!)

8-WEEK STUDY GUIDE

by
CARTER FEATHERSTON

WORD & SPIRIT
PUBLISHING

God Knows Your Story . . . and He's Not Mad!
8-Week Study Guide
ISBN: 978-1-949106-36-7
Copyright © 2020 by Carter Featherston

Published by Word and Spirit Publishing
P.O. Box 701403
Tulsa, Oklahoma 74170
wordandspiritpublishing.com

CONTENTS

WORD OF CAUTION to
Small Group Leaders

Thank you for your leadership and courage
to pick up the book, *God Knows Your Story, and He's Not Mad!*
and lead a group of people through this study.
People's lives will change as they work through
these questions week to week.

If your participants are going to get the most out of this work,
they will be guided to go back to some painful
and hurtful episodes from their past.
They might uncover some very shameful memories.
Many of the participants will struggle to recall this pain alone with God,
but hopefully their prayer work with Him will be liberating!
However, they will not want to share this very personal work
publicly at the group meetings.
PLEASE RESPECT THEIR BOUNDARIES.
Help these people feel safe.
Let everyone know each week, that no one has to re-tell
publicly any part of their story that they are not ready to tell.
This means, for you as the leader, you will need to
prayerfully decide before each group meeting
which questions you will invite everyone to discuss,
and which questions some people can remain silent for,
if they are not comfortable discussing that part of their story.

May the Lord bless your individual study time
and your group discussions, for the growth of
everyone involved, and to the glory of God!

Introduction

From a casual reading of the Bible, we see that God is a story-teller. The Bible is one big story of how He came to redeem us from the mess that we were in, but within that big story there are hundreds of smaller stories. Much of the Bible is stories—true stories—of men and women struggling with the difficulties of life. Some of those stories allow God to work His grace, while some of those stories end in tragedy. Today, we also struggle with what life has handed us, what others have done to us, and how our hearts and minds are broken by it, all of which needs redemptive healing.

As part of the story, God made us to be storytellers, too. He made us to be relational so that we could have a walking, talking relationship with Him, as well as with our fellow story characters. He designed us to be conversational and questioning human beings, so that He could dialogue with us about His purposes in our lives. He comes to us as our Redeemer, to change the direction of our stories, and He walks with us as our Healer, to set us free from the damage in our stories. Ever since the Garden of Eden (*Genesis 2*), He has been longing for us to have intimacy with Him in—and despite—our story.

However, that intimacy has been hindered by our sin and broken-ness, and the painful memories of our stories. Something went wrong in the Garden story (*Genesis 3*), and something has gone wrong in our stories, too. Instead of intimacy, there is aloneness. Instead of growth, we hit a wall. Instead of peace, there is anger and fear. God wants to meet us in the painful memories of our stories that have us stuck. Not because He's mad, but because He wants to start a dialogue with us to bring healing to our hearts and redeem the broken places of our lives. He wants to change us, so that we can join with Him to help change others with stories like ours.

God is continuously creating and engaging us in every chapter of our lives. He knows our stories, and He wants us to know and understand them, too, lest we miss His eternal purposes for us. However, most of us ignore our stories, or we discount the past. We don't understand our stories, so we fail to engage God meaningfully. Dan Allender laments, "*We often tell our stories poorly. We tell our stories without curiosity and create only boredom. We tell them without honesty . . . We tell them without gentleness and weave tales of vengeance against ourselves and others. By telling our stories poorly, we dishonor them and mire ourselves in anger and contempt.*"[1]

If we don't join God to take control of our stories, our stories will always control us. It may be painful to go back and revisit the past, especially if we go back alone. But the purpose of this book is to show you how to go back with God through storytelling prayer work. Again, Allender points out, "*One of the privileges of being human is that we have an enormous capacity to reflect and learn and change . . . Choosing a richer life requires revisiting the past, which may reopen painful wounds and failure and betrayal. The only reason worth reentering that pain is the hope that somehow it can be transformed, that through it we will learn to love better and we will know more joy.*"[2] There is a reason you are on this earth. That reason includes what you have had to go through in life. God wants to use you in His redemptive work in others. But He wants to introduce others to the hope of healing, by healing you first. This study is designed to introduce you to a process in which God will grace your heart with freedom and power, then change the trajectory of your story. Afterward, you can join Him in this transforming work for other people whose stories are much like yours.

---

[1] Dan B. Allender and Lisa K. Fann, *To Be Told, Workbook* (Colorado Springs: Waterbrook Press, 2005), 1.

[2] Ibid., 2.

Chapters 1–4

What's in Your Story?

Home is where your story begins. Home is where you are born into a story already with a context, a context of other ongoing stories. Your mother and father came together, living in their own stories. Your parents started a family, for better or for worse, that would be shaped directly by what had already happened in their own lives, in the events and memories that happened long before you were born. Early in your life, their context controlled much of what you experienced. Their stories set the course for your life, and that course often points to the purposes that God has for you in order to build up His Church. That is, your unique ministry will be built around the particular story you have lived and what you have gone through, including, of course, the triumph you have found in Christ's healing presence.

1. Identify several positive gifts from God in your life. (For example, one or both of your parents, an amazing childhood event, a grandparent, a teacher, a pet, a best friend, a vacation, any accomplishments you have achieved with your God-given talents, etc.)

I realize that God was good to me by blessing me with . . .

2. Identify two or three negative memories from your early childhood up through the sixth grade, or age twelve. (For example,
did you suffer abuse of any kind? Were you mocked or
ridiculed, rejected by friend(s), or humiliated by a teacher or
coach? Were you body-shamed, or did you experience the death
of a loved one? Did your family move, causing you to leave
friends and become the new kid starting at a new school?)

*I acknowledge that some of the greatest sadness in my child-
hood came from . . .*

3. Identify the grace of God in His provision for you during this same
time period. Did He provide a loving relative, teacher, friend, or
parent of a friend to show you His love and care for you? Can you
remember and write about one particular memory?

*After a painful event in life, I now realize that God brought
love, acceptance, comfort, and/or friendship through (this*

person) _____. *Here's how they loved/comforted me:*

4. *From Hiding to Honesty.* The first chapter of the book began with the idea that we are hiding. We hide our stories from others because we are minimizing them to ourselves. This is self-deception, at worst; or a lack of self-awareness, at the least. A long-ago definition of *honesty* was "free from fraud." To be honest is to be truthful, to own your story, the true story of your life with no self-deception.

One painful memory from my childhood story that I tend to minimize, discount, disregard, or fully avoid thinking about is . . .

One painful memory from my childhood that tended to repeat itself is . . .

5. If God is always asking questions, what question might you be avoiding? Can you identify a conflict hidden behind your internal monologue (make use of questions 2 and 4 above) that needs to be dealt with in an honest dialogue with God?

   One question that I need to resolve with God about my early childhood is . . .

6. If you were a news correspondent writing a biographical sketch for your readers, what headline would you write for this early part of your life? (For example: "Ten-Year-Old's Parents Divorce: Left Feeling Alone and Unloved"; "Forgotten After Ball Practice: Nine-Year-Old Scared and Alone at the Park, Pattern Repeats"; "Entering the Fifth Grade in the Fourth New School; Ten-Year-Old Always Feels Alone"; "Parents Fighting Again: Six-Year-Old Alone in Bed and God Is Nowhere to Be Found"; "Happy in Life: Sixth-Grader's Success Always Feels Like Never Enough"; etc.)

Chapters 5–7

God Wants a Conversation

Nowhere in Scripture does God reason like a psychologist as well as He does in Romans 1:18–32. He makes it very clear that if you do not cleanse your heart in dialogue with Him, eventually you will stop being worshipful and grateful, and worse, your heart will get darker. God reveals to us that the way of spiritual growth with a pure heart is to cleanse our heart through dialogue. No dialogue, then no cleansing. However, don't mistakenly think that God is full of anger and condemnation about your sin and your story. No, He has a greater plan, but it is not merely to get you to stop sinning. His plan is to diminish the power of shame over your life and establish you in the righteousness of your new identity in Christ.

1. Read through Paul's terrible list of sins in Romans 1:28–32. Can you identify a few sins from this list that you were guilty of during your teenage and young adult years?

2. Of the Ten Commandments found in the Law of Moses, only the fifth commandment is repeated verbatim in the New Covenant: *"Honor your father and mother"* *(this is the first commandment with promise)* *"that it may go well with you and that you may live long on the earth"* *(Ephesians 6:2–3 ESV)*. Can you name any way in which you dishonored your parents? Has this affected your health in any way, emotionally, physically, or spiritually? Would you be willing to set a time of prayer with the Father to acknowledge these sins, renounce the attitudes, and be healed of this unfinished business?

3. One of the major points made in the book is that many of today's stubborn, stronghold behaviors come from yesterday's unhealed wounds. Can you identify the internal conflicts *(family issues, school troubles, relationship conflicts, etc.)* that influenced you to walk in the sins you just identified in question 1? In other words, what was driving you internally in your youth *(anger about something at home; fear; feeling ashamed; feeling like a failure)*?

4. The author described an old wound in his past that created these internal conflicts for him. It was the event at the school lunchroom table in the fifth grade, where his life changed forever. Do you remember a day in your life when something painful or unsettling happened, and a defeating message arose in your heart? Was there a day when something negative (perhaps, even devastating) happened, and you knew life would never be the same again? Can you write a few sentences describing this event? *(If you have already identified it above, amplify it with more of your thoughts here.)*

5. Which of the Scripture passages identified in Chapter 6 of the book was the most revealing to you, to help you understand that God is not mad at you? Can you identify any other statements by the author in Chapter 6 that provide comfort?

6. If you don't learn to tell your story from the perspective of God's redemptive work in your story, then Shame will tell another story. Does your own shame manifest in the words of your self-talk when you make a mistake? Identify any negative, shameful messages that you say to yourself.

   When I make mistakes in life, I berate myself by saying . . .

   When I have let other people down, I judge myself by saying . . .

   When I fail at something, I condemn myself by saying . . .

7. Read 2 Corinthians 2:11. It appears that Satan has a short-range plan for your life. His strategy is to keep you defeated by whispering your life story back to you with the message of shame as his theme. As your enemy, he wants you to feel Ashamed, Defeated, Damaged, a Failure, Selfish, and Stupid, to name a few. In our workplaces, we have weekly reports to fill out (for sales, inventory, or progress on a project, for example). Can you imagine if the enemy had to turn in a weekly report at staff meetings in hell? Can you make up in your mind what his report about you might have said back in your teen years (based on your answers above)?

Work Report: *"Having observed the painful events in the life of my 'subject,' here is an update on what I am scheming to accomplish in his/her life. I am working to get **this shameful message** repeated in his/her life:*

Chapters 8–10

How Shame Develops and Reinforces Itself

The reason Shame is such a soul-eater is that it is not a mere passing feeling, or a passing emotion. It's worse than that. Shame is an identity. We construct our own unique version of Shame memory by memory, event by event, pain by pain. As the identity of shame develops within us, it is entrenched by our own coping mechanisms and sins we use to hide (the flesh). A further part of our flesh is the posturing and posing of a false self, a false personality that we try to "shop around" to others at work and in the church, so they have no idea how deep our shame runs. *"Shame tends to be self-reinforcing"* (Curt Thompson, *The Soul of Shame,* p. 31).

1. Looking back at your school years (grades 1–12), is there a memory of either of your parents, a teacher, a coach, or another adult who went beyond calling out your sin (behavior) and declared an identity over you? (For example, consider the

story in the book of the principal calling the young student a Liar.) Tell your story briefly here.

2. When people are first introduced to the idea of Shame, many discount it or even dismiss it. If you ask, most people will deny any shame and claim that they do not hate themselves or hate anything about themselves. But shame is the inheritance of all descendants of Adam and Eve. It is a universal condition into which all of us are born. Can you identify any of your self-talk at the different levels of Shame?

   a. *At the shallow level of Shame, here is something that I didn't like about how God made me:*

   "I am not _____ enough."

   b. *At the middle level of Shame, I can recognize today that there were things about my behavior, or my performance, that indicated that I did not respect myself.*

"I am too/so _____" (something negative).

c. *Here is how it shows up today in my adult self-talk (cf. question 6 from last week):*

"I will never be _____."

"I can't _____."

"I can't ever be _____."

"I just hate it when I _____."

"I'm such a _____."

3. On page 66, the author describes how Shame begins to heal. Rewrite in your own words the beginning of this healing process:

4. Your Purpose-Driven Life.

    a. For some of us, our purpose-driven life included being fantastic rule-keepers. We complied with our parents, we obeyed the rules, we turned in homework on time, and we lived up to the expectations that others had of us. What if all of this perfect behavior was actually energized by fear? What if this behavior was more driven by people-pleasing as a way to manipulate approval? The fear of failure is a sign that shame is controlling you from a deeper place in the soul. If this was you, can you now identify the shame behind this dutiful obedience?

    I was very attentive to my studies, my chores, my rule-following. My parents and teachers were always proud of me. However, today I recognize that I was driven by fear. Here is what I was afraid of:

    b. For others of us, our purpose-driven life was to be a rebel. We loved the slogan, "Rules are made to be broken," and so we did! We were stubborn and defiant; we had to have it our way. Do you recognize today that this behavior was driven by anger?

Here is what I was angry about:

5. Your purpose-driven life comes from your mind-set on how to get your needs met for love and acceptance. Based on the negative identity emerging in your soul, you purposely developed your own unique version of the Flesh. The Flesh is your strategy (apart from God) to cope and deal with life as it is showing up. The author's full definition of *Flesh* is this: *All the ways (apart from God) that I Protect myself, Provide for myself, Promote myself, and Pleasure myself.* What were the behaviors and attitudes of your purpose-driven life (your *Flesh*) growing up?

I protected myself by . . .

I provided for myself with . . .

I promoted myself by . . .

I pleasured myself with . . .

6. The cover up of Shame is complete when we develop a *False Self.* This is the personality we send out in public to fool people about how we really feel about ourselves. *Who were you? How did you want people to perceive you?* Can you put a nametag on yourself that describes your false self, the image that you hoped others would accept as the real you? Then below the name, write out in parentheses what you were really hiding.

(Remember, the Shame-based identity is the name and identity you started to recognize in question 6 in Week 1 and question 6 in Week 2. The nametag below will be the outward person you developed to hide your true story. For example: "Hello, my name is Mr. Hilarious (who really feels unloved)"; "Pretty (but empty)"; "Little Miss Perfect (afraid to have my mistakes pointed out)"; "Macho Man (who's actually afraid)"; "Funny

Girl (who's hiding my abused heart)"; "Mr. Confidence (who feels phony)"; "Smartest Man in the Room (hiding my need to be right)"; "Fashion Model (who actually feels ugly)"; "Ice Queen—leave me alone! (hiding my self-hatred)"; "Junkyard Dog—stand back! (hiding my abusive home)"; "Goody, Goody Church Kid (hiding my secrets)"; etc.

HELLO

MY NAME IS

(_____)

Chapters 11–13

Healing Begins with Spirit-Taught Truth

A biblical psychology of man must always include the distinction between the spirit and the soul. We are spirit-beings, and the spirit is the locus of our identity, the location where God has shared His righteous life with us. We have a valuable and powerful new relationship with God *in our spirit*. The first and primary work of the Holy Spirit in our lives is to teach us this distinction between spirit and soul, and to confirm to us that we are children of our Father God. This way, we know who we are, and we don't spend our lives trying to become who we already are.

1. Which Scripture references and explanations by the author were most illuminating for you to see the difference between the spirit and the soul? *Write out your own understanding of this difference to help cement it in your mind.*

2. When we say that our identity is in Christ, do you have a fuller understanding now of what that means from chapter 12? The location of our identity is in the spirit. Whatever life is in your spirit, that is your identity. You are either still in Adam, or your spirit has been born again and you are in Christ. If He is your life (see Colossians 3:4) in your spirit, then He is your identity. Read the first full paragraph on page 108 of the book. In a few sentences below, can you process what that paragraph is telling you?

3. In your adolescence and high school years, how did you live to secure your own sense of Value, Goodness, and Power?

4. **Your Story versus Christ's Life; Soul versus Spirit.** In the diagram below, inside the "soul" and "spirit," write out the descriptions that fit for each. To get you started, we have suggested one description for the soul and one description for the spirit from Ephesians 1. Fill in words for *your* soul based on your answers about your life story from above. Then, from Ephesians 1:3-14, fill in words for the spirit that could heal your heart. Draw a line between the labels in the soul and words in the spirit, connecting the spiritual truths that cancel out the shame in the soul. *(Let the chart on page 112 help you.)*

5. Suppose you lived in Ephesus in the first century. Suppose you were sitting in the home where the apostle Paul was teaching the content of Ephesians 1:3–14. After telling you that you have a Value, a Goodness, a Power, and Authority in Christ, suppose that he stopped teaching to tell you that he wanted to dismiss the crowd so he could be alone to pray. Read his prayer in 1:16–21. Based on these verses, how does Paul tell us that we learn our new identity?

6. What does the author mean when he talks about making a change at the level of Identity?

WEEK 5

Chapters 14–15

How Shame Emerged in Your Own Personal Story

M ost of the pain in our lives can be analyzed under three broad categories. We have the emptiness and loneliness of HOLES; the shock and trauma from WOUNDS; and the gut-wrenching pain from ARROWS of rejection. Then we make these three dimensions worse with our own faulty thinking. Our shame-based identity emerges in our faulty thinking about this pain. Breaking this down from an emotional standpoint with the Emotional Cup diagram can be illuminating. Hopefully, you will see your own story even more clearly through this exercise.

1. If intimacy was scarce in your home when you were growing up, what was not scarce? That is, what contributed to any pain and lack of intimacy in your family?

23

2. Think of your early home life during your adolescence and teenage years. You have many painful memories. Can you identify which of the three categories of Pain they would fit under?

HOLES: *Here is a short list of memories from when I felt neglected, abandoned, ignored, left out, left behind . . .*

WOUNDS: *Here is a short list of memories from when I was hurt, shamed, emasculated, ridiculed, belittled, mocked . . .*

REJECTIONS: *Here are several severe rejections that I felt from my peers, or a boyfriend/girlfriend, or from an ex-spouse . . .*

3. *Hiding Behind Lies.* Can you now see that your shame is built around Lies, the Fault Lines in your soul? In all of this reflection on your life, can you now identify four to six Lies that you adopted in life? (For example: Lies about God, Lies about life, Lies about yourself, Lies about love, Lies about family, Lies about trusting, etc.)

One lie that I tell myself about my early childhood is . . .

One lie that I came to believe about myself is . . .

A lie that I believed about love/friendship/acceptance is . . .

A lie that I believed about my image is . . .

One lie that I wrongly believed about God is . . .

(REMEMBER: It might be *true* that your life *was* sad; *true* that your father *was* an abusive alcoholic; *true* that your mother *was* self-absorbed and neglectful; *true* that you *were* rejected. But it's *not true*, therefore, that you are Worthless forever, or that you are Damaged Goods, or that you will Never Be Loved, or that you will always be a Reject. Your story does not have to be your Identity! Your story is *what happened.* Your shame is *what you decided wrongly that it means about you.*)

4. Which portion of the Emotional Cup controls your life the most? What is the cause of it in your story?

5. Growing up, how did you seek comfort from the discomfort and what was accumulating in your emotional cup?

6. Today, in your role as a spouse, or parent, or leader in business, how do you seek comfort from the hurt in your cup?

7. God wants to deliver and transform you from the "comfort-seeking" behaviors that flow from the toxic emotions in your emotional cup. Where in the emotional cup does He want to begin your transformation?

Chapters 16–17

Grace and the Restoration Plan

L aw implies that I must do something for God; Grace implies that God will do something for me. We spend too much of our Christian lives oriented toward achieving instead of receiving. Grace is not about idleness, although it is about waiting (see Isaiah 40:31). Grace is not about self-effort, though it does include energy. Grace is not about accomplishment; but is more about enablement. Grace is a process of *revelation, response,* and *results.* God reveals to us something that needs to change. We receive that revelation and respond with faith. Then, as we are controlled by the Holy Spirit in regard to the matter, grace brings about results. The journey of healing the Christian soul starts with the revelation that God's great and perfect love comes to us as comfort from Him, allowing us to put away our anger, as fear is cast out. All of this leads to a deeper intimacy with the Father, Son, and Holy Spirit as we walk the journey together.

1. Can you write out the two definitions of Grace presented in Chapter 16?

   Grace 1:

   Grace 2:

2. Reread the paragraph that starts on the bottom of page 159 and runs through the top of page 160. The author says that we use a lot of vocabulary not found in the New Testament. Is he right? Think about your vocabulary, and the vocabulary you hear in the church pews about "what to do to grow as a Christian." In exhorting ourselves and our friends in spiritual growth, can you list any words or phrases used that also are not found in the New Testament? Have you used any of the words that the author identified? Do you agree with his point?

3. Take your Bible and read the description of the New Covenant in Ezekiel 36:25–27. (Do not use a paraphrase, but use a standard word-for-word translation of the Bible, such as the NIV, ESV, NASB, NKJV, etc.) List everything in those three verses that God says He will do:

God says, "I will . . .

Now, write out what God says that we are to do:

4. Interesting, isn't it? There is nothing specifically outlined for us to do in this description of the New Covenant. God is going to do all of it. He even says He will *make* or *cause* us to obey Him. Do you believe that? Strictly from these three verses only (don't look anywhere else in Scripture), *how and with what* does God cause us to obey Him?

5. Today's stubborn sins come from yesterday's unhealed wounds. If Grace is going to deliver us from our stubborn sins, then Grace must also heal our wounds. Law can do neither. In fact, living under Law will only keep your sins alive. One purpose of Romans 7 is to teach us that Law will no longer work for spiritual growth. In fact, what does Romans 7:13 tell us will happen if we go backward and use the law to fight our sin struggle?

6. Consider this: If you are focused on the law, then you will always be focused on your self-performance. If you are always focused on your self-performance, then you will always be focused on your successes or failures. If you are always focused on you, this is known as what (see Luke 18:9; Galatians 5:4; Isaiah 64:6)?

7. Take your Bible and read Titus 2:11–12. Notice the verbs in these two verses: *has appeared* and *training*. The actions of "appearing" and "training" sound like Grace is a Person—the

WEEK 6 – **Chapters 16–17** | Grace and the Restoration Plan

person of Christ, of course. Christ appears to us like an epiphany and we are born again, and then Christ trains us to walk in godliness. The author uses this phrase on page 159: *"I walked, He worked."*

    a. Do you think this phrase is biblical? Can you amplify what you think the author means?

    b. Grace doesn't mean that I don't have to do anything. It does mean that I don't achieve my own righteousness. Rather, I walk in a righteousness I possess from God. In the Grace-system what is the fundamental and first requirement of us? (Make use of Romans 6:12–13; Romans 12:1; Hebrews 13:9.)

8. According to the author (see pages 166–167), where does God want to meet us to deliver us from our stubborn sin patterns? Do you agree with this? Could this explain why so many in the Church never overcome their stubborn sins?

9. In a sad, painful time in your life, did God ever come to you in a tangible way to comfort you? Can you briefly tell the story here?

10. In your life experience, has forgiveness ever been a long, long journey that seemed to take forever? Forgiving an offender is difficult issue because we cannot be rid of our anger at their offense. On page 173, the author makes the point that this difficulty is because we first do not receive the comfort of God for the pain of the other's offense. We try to forgive the person who hurt us *before* we have been healed by God's comfort. We try to deal with the Anger before we first deal with the Pain. Do you think this is biblical, that intimate comfort from God precedes active forgiveness for others? That is, does Intimacy precede Activity? Why or why not?

Chapters 18–19

Healing Prayer and Taking a New Stand

Where did your shame come from? . . . From this memory, this memory, this memory, that memory, that memory, and the other memory you are trying to forget about. Your shame came from your backstory of pain, from your abandonment, neglect, wounds, beatdowns, rejections, and betrayals (to name a few). So, the next question would be, how do you heal your shame? By praying in the Spirit about this memory, this memory, that memory, that memory, and the other memory you are trying to forget about; as well as from every memory of abandonment, neglect, wounding, beatdown, rejection, and betrayal (to name a few). Your shame accumulated from one hurtful memory to the next. So, your healing will come by taking one hurtful memory to the next into the throne room of God to receive His comfort, His healing, and His renovation of your heart. We overcome shame when we receive our healing, and then we begin to reign over our backstory, speaking our authority in Christ.

God Knows Your Story . . . and He's Not Mad! | **8-Week Study Guide**

1. When you and God can get time alone, write in your journal about one of the painful memories from your childhood/teen years. Then walk with Christ through that memory following the Prayer Guide found in Chapter 18.

   If you need help, start a dialogue with God using the following questions:

   a. Who do You want me to be in life? Who do I want to be in my home/relationships?

   b. What is the major emotion standing in my way?

   c. What, then, is the lie I am believing? What lie is attached to this emotion?

   d. How far back in life did I first start believing this lie? What memory holds this lie?

2. For your homework this week, we encourage you to get alone with God two or three more times and take other memories through the Healing Prayer Guide found in Chapter 18.

36

3. Can you identify two or three close friends with whom you can share some or part of your story? Now that you have begun to understand your story, and you have done some healing with the prayer exercise, who could you get with over coffee to share what God is doing to transform you at the level of identity? Name them here:

    a.

    b.

    c.

4. Do you live as a victim in any area of your life? Be honest. Is there a relationship, a situation, or a conflict in which you are passive, but you blame others for being selfish, aggressive, bossy, or "bullies"? Or are *you* the bully? Do you dish out on others from the pain you received as a victim earlier in life? What would your loved ones say about you?

    a. *I live as a victim when . . .*

b. *I live as a bully when . . .*

c. *If my loved ones gave me honest feedback, they would say this about me . . .*

5. You cannot change or heal what you do not acknowledge. What would your loved ones say are your bad traits? If what they say is true, what is it that you need to acknowledge about your life (your sin patterns, your secrets, your self-judgments, your critical spirit toward others, etc.)? Thus, what memory from your story still reigns over you?

6. Who do you know in life that functions in the office of a king? Who do you know in life that has overcome their story and helps other believers to live healthier in Christ? *(Write their names below.)*

   Here are individuals who come to mind that I admire for walking as kings under the King of Kings, who have overcome their story and are helpful to others:

   a.

   b.

   c.

7. Do you also want to walk in such power and authority? Are you ready to take seriously the healing of your soul so that you might **"reign in life through the one man, Jesus Christ"** *(Romans 5:17)?* What are the barriers standing in the way? What do you need to do about these barriers?

   a. Here is the more important healing that I need in order to walk in authority:

b. Here are the barriers that stand in the way of my healing:

c. Here is what I need to do about it:

8. Is there an inkling in your heart of a mission God might have for you? Is there a way God might want to use you, if you let Him finish this healing journey?

Chapters 20–22

Reigning with Authority and Grace to Break Through

Our identity in Christ includes His authority. He has seated you in heavenly places, upon His throne with Him (see Ephesians 2:6), and anyone who sits on a throne has authority. With this authority, it is time for us to no longer allow our thoughts and emotions to have control over us, but it is time for us to have control over them. We take control over them by recognizing/hearing them in our mind, taking them captive to Christ, and cancelling them out with our declarations of biblical truth. We speak the truth. We speak our righteousness. We speak our triumph. We speak what we believe! And the Lord of the Breakthrough will grant us a wonder-working grace that will deliver us from our covenant with death.

1. If you have been mindful and diligent with all the work in the previous seven weeks, then you should well be able to recognize the shame-based lies and labels from your childhood that you still speak to yourself. The renewing of your mind takes

active diligence, as we must "take every thought captive to obey Christ" (2 Corinthians 10:5). Write out, again, five or six negative messages you tell yourself.

a.

b.

c.

d.

e.

Now take each ungodly belief and shameful message individually through this prayer:

Dear Lord Jesus, thank You for Your healing presence, which renews my mind. I renounce the message that _____; I renounce it as a lie, and I reject it from my mind. In Your name. Amen.

2. Many of us have undesirable images that play in our minds. The Bible calls them the "useless speculations" of monologue (Romans 1:21 NASB). We make up in our minds fantasies of "payback conversations" in which this time we give people "a piece of our mind"; we make up steamy romantic fantasies, or acts of revenge. We also have *true-life* memories of hurtful conversations, regrettable actions, past sexual behaviors, or troubling violence in our past. These memories can sully our attitudes, condemn our hearts, keep us ashamed, or keep us agitated and absent of the peace of Christ.

    Take some time this week to sit quietly before the Lord and ask Him if there are any such hurtful images active in your mind (see Psalm 139:24). As He reveals the vindictive videos, the shameful episodes, the sexual escapades, or the grimacing violence that plays in your mind, remove their haunting or harassing presence from your mind with the following prayer. See each scene, every detail that is real or a made up fantasy, and follow the illustration of Sandy on page 210 of the book. (Make use also of point *e.* on page 184 of the book.) Ask the Holy Spirit to bring to your mind all images that have a negative impact on your spiritual, emotional, and mental health. As the images begin to surface renounce each picture or memory as they emerge and pray the following prayer . . .

    I renounce that image . . . I renounce that image . . . I renounce that image . . . (until no more images arise; then pray . . .)

    Lord Jesus, I cast all these images from my mind, and I ask You to cleanse my mind from all unrighteousness. In the power of Your name I pray. Amen.

3. In the strategy for taking control over your mind and emotions (page 214), why is it sometimes necessary to start with identifying your emotions first?

4. Spiritual maturity is incomplete without emotional awareness. The strategy on pages 215-217 present a tool that should be practiced for the rest of your life. For extra homework this week, take time to slowly read through the strategy on pages 215–217 and make a mental note to practice feeling your emotions in the days ahead. Feel your anger or melancholy at the end of the workday and see if you can trace that emotion back to your thinking earlier in the day. Can you discover the "telegram?"

   Below, write about your experience doing this, and answer this question: Why would God want me to be aware of my emotions throughout the day?

5. To be made in the image of God is to be a creative, speaking, ruling being—just as God is. The angels are powerful creatures, but, according to the author in Chapter 21, what power does God give us that He does not give them?

6. We worship a God who calls into existence the things that do not exist (Romans 4:17). He gives us a measure of this same power, that is, to speak with our mouths the power of His Word. We can call His Word and Spirit into our lives to change the direction of our stories. Based on your life's circumstances right now, with which word in 2 Corinthians 4:8–9 would you most identify? Are you *afflicted*? Are you *perplexed*? Are you *persecuted*? Or do you feel *struck down*?

What do you need to believe and speak now? Do any of the Scripture verses on pages 224–226 fit your circumstances and speak to your heart? Could one of these verses call faith into your heart where it does not exist? Rewrite that verse here in your own words. Use other translations to help amplify the verse.

Can you find another verse in the Bible to read, believe, and speak that would be useful for your situation? Write it below to help you remember or even memorize it.

7. Did you find yourself in agreement with the author (pages 234–235) about the story in John 5? That is, have you also thought that Jesus' question to the man at the Pool of Bethesda was strange? Of course, everyone at that pool wanted to get well! But let's apply this story to you. Is it possible that you do not want to get well? (Be honest, for your own sake!) Is it possible that you have a covenant-like attachment to some stubborn sin in your life, and that long ago you lost the determination to address it with God? (For example, a critical spirit,

unforgiveness toward someone in particular, self-promotion, always talking, a secret lust, sneaky drinking or overeating, etc. Do you have to be the most popular person in the room? Do you have to be the smartest person in the room? Do you act superior? Do you always make judgments about others?)

What would your family say is your stubborn bad trait?

What greater grace (see James 4:6) would you need from God to enable you to experience a breakthrough?

What would be your answer to Christ if He personally asked you, "What do you want Me to do for you in regard to this stubborn stronghold in your life?" Would you make a covenant in your heart with God that you will remain focused and attentive to this issue, until His grace has led you in triumph over this area of your life?

Lord Jesus, I agree with you about the stronghold of _____ _____ that has reigned long enough in my life. I want to take a walk of grace with you in regard to this, and use the tools from this book and other tools you reveal to me, to attend to this matter faithfully, until you and I are walking out of it in triumph together. Amen.

FINAL THOUGHTS

Did anything in your life change during this study?

Has there been a shift in your life from anything you addressed in your backstory during this study? We hope so!

We hope that you gave considerable weight of thought and prayer during these eight weeks; that you experienced a deeper working of the Holy Spirit; that you are walking in a greater freedom in Christ.

This was our goal with this book and the study guide: to take your knowledge of Scripture and go deeper into a study of you, a deeper study of your story and how your own unique version of shame developed; then to give you a prayer guide for working through the healing of the "unfinished business" of your backstory.

If you ever wish to return to the *big idea of GOD KNOWS YOUR STORY, and He's Not Mad!* you can find a summary of that theme on pages 229–231. On these first two and a half pages of Chapter 22, the author lays out an explanation of the spiritual journey that he is encouraging us to recognize and address. If someone were interested in knowing what this book is about, you could hand them your copy and suggest that they read these two and a half pages to see if it creates an interest in the theme of this book and the work of this study guide.

The author, Carter Featherston, is also available to conduct a Pure Heart Weekend at your church. You can read more about the weekend on his website. Talk with your pastor about the idea and have your pastor contact Carter to discuss his schedule and his ideas on planning this retreat in your particular situation. The retreat can be done in an all-woman format or an all-men format, and the work we do often goes straight to the heart of the matter where your spiritual life is stalled-out or where your marriage is struggling. The weekend can be a solid support for healing and restoration in your church.

A Pure Heart Weekend is also a great tool for a leadership retreat for church teams. Working together on your stories is a great way to strengthen your love and support for one another on pastoral staffs, ministry teams, or a church board.

Carter Featherston
B.A. Wheaton College
Th.M. Dallas Theological Seminary

Founder of
RESTORE ONE, Inc
"Helping believers change at the level of Identity"
www.carterfeatherston.com
email him at: carter@carterfeatherston.com

BIO

Carter Featherston, Th.M.

Restore One Ministries

Website: http://www.carterfeatherston.com

Carter Featherston is a pastoral-counselor, retreat leader and speaker. He leads a retreat for spiritual transformation called Pure Heart Weekend, through which he has helped hundreds of people change at the level of identity through life mapping, healing prayer and breaking strongholds. Carter is also the author of the eBook, *God Knows Your Struggle; and He Wants to Help* (Amazon), a book on breaking the control of sexual strongholds and shame. He and his wife, Cindy, have three adult children and two grandchildren. He and Cindy live in Covington, LA with their two dogs, Sami and Zoey.